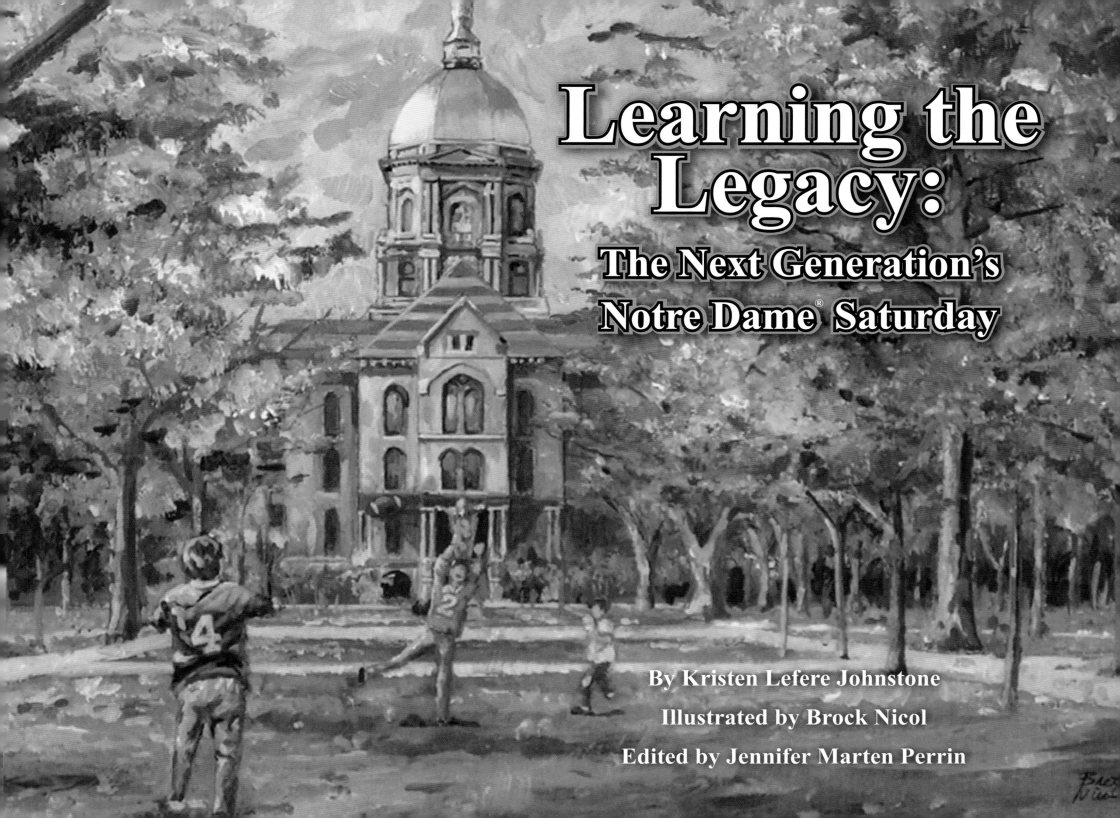

Learning the Legacy:
The Next Generation's Notre Dame® Saturday

By Kristen Lefere Johnstone

Illustrated by Brock Nicol

Edited by Jennifer Marten Perrin

Acknowledgements

So many people graciously helped in the process of making this book a reality. To Ted Lefere, Mike Wigton, Ed Ledford, Aaron Rachelson, Kaija (Clark) Wadsworth, Brad Miller, Carrie Hood, Steve Camilleri, Bethany Riddle, Jim Langford, Sue Shidler at the Hammes Bookstore, and Mike Low and Tomi Gerhold in Notre Dame Licensing: Your expertise, assistance, and patience were a tremendous help. Brock, I couldn't be happier with the art or with the whole experience of working together. Marten, you're an amazing editor, researcher, and friend; I could not have done this without you. To the extended Lefere, Roberts, Johnstone, and Wentling families: Thank you for all your support. Finally, I am indebted to my parents Jerry and Carol Lefere, my friend Amy Wentling Birmingham, and especially my husband Sean for their endless patience and encouragement.

KLJ Productions, Inc.

http://www.LearningTheLegacy.com

Illustrations completed by Brock Nicol.
For more information, contact www.creativeshake.com/brocknicol or brockdraw@sympatico.ca

Book Design and Layout created by:
Brad Miller Design, 2144 N. Claremont, Chicago, IL 60647, (773) 334-4814, www.bradmillerdesign.com

"Play Like A Champion Today" is used with the limited permission of Play Like A Champion Today, Inc.
Knute Rockne image used with permission of Rockne Enterprises, c/o CMG Worldwide, Inc.
TM/©2008 Knute Rockne by CMG Worldwide/ www.CMGWorldwide.com

ISBN 978-0-9815536-0-3

For Mom and Dad, who taught me,

And for Jack and Jessie, who I hope will learn.

One bright, crisp, autumn day in South Bend in September,

My father taught me lessons that I always will remember.

We'd come to see the Irish play, and he gently took my hand.

He said, "There are some things that I want you to understand.

It's far too much to learn today. There's so much here to see.

I'll just do the best I can; we'll go from A to Z."

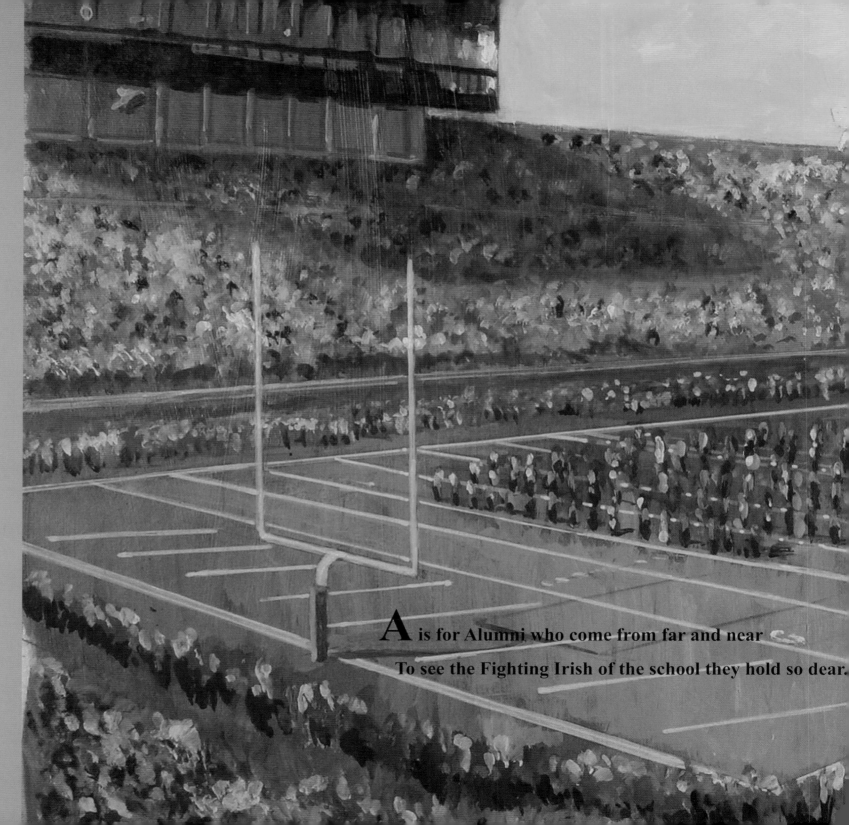

A a

Notre Dame is blessed with a proud and active alumni population. Graduates can find over 250 local alumni clubs, including over 50 international clubs. With so many Domers spread across the world, football Saturdays often serve as mini-reunions for classmates and friends. Although nearly half of the Notre Dame Stadium seats are reserved for students and alumni, demand is so high that a yearly lottery must be held to distribute tickets to alumni.

A is for Alumni who come from far and near
To see the Fighting Irish of the school they hold so dear.

B is for the members of the nation's oldest Band.
When they play the fight song, sing as loudly as you can.

Bb

The Band of the Fighting Irish was formed in 1845, making it the oldest university band in continual existence. Since 1887, the band has played for every home football game. Approximately 380 students from the University of Notre Dame, Saint Mary's College, and Holy Cross College form the core of the band today. Members of the band are not awarded scholarships; instead, they voluntarily devote their time, energy, and considerable talents to serve the University.

C c

C is for the Coaches
who have ended the year number one:
Rockne, Leahy, Parseghian, Devine,
Holtz — and more to come.

Five Notre Dame coaches
have led their teams
to consensus national
championships: Knute
Rockne in 1924, 1929, and
1930; Frank Leahy in 1943,
1946, 1947, and 1949; Ara
Parseghian in 1966 and
1973; Dan Devine in 1977;
and Lou Holtz in 1988.

D is for the Golden Dome, where
Mary has her view,
Watching over the Irish when they
wear Our Lady's blue.

Dd

Thanks to the persistence of
Reverend Edward F. Sorin,
C.S.C., the Golden Dome
of the Main Building rises
above campus as Notre
Dame's most recognizable
landmark. When the original
Main Building burned in
1879, Father Sorin, the
school's founder, insisted
a larger building be
constructed and topped
with a golden dome in honor
of the Virgin Mary. Today,
the Dome and 16 foot tall
statue of Mary are gilded
with 3,500 square feet of
23.9 carat gold.

E e

Sportswriter Grantland Rice wrote the Four Horsemen into sports history with the first line of his October 19, 1924 *New York Herald-Tribune* story about Notre Dame's 13-7 victory over Army:

"Outlined against a blue, gray October sky the Four Horsemen rode again. In dramatic lore they are known as famine, pestilence, destruction and death. These are only aliases. Their real names are: Stuhldreher, Miller, Crowley and Layden."

Quarterback Harry Stuhldreher, left halfback Jim Crowley, right halfback Don Miller, and fullback Elmer Layden were perhaps the greatest backfield in the history of college football. In 1924, they led Notre Dame to its first national championship and an undefeated record. Individually, they are each members of the College Football Hall of Fame.

E is for the Echoes that still sound from long ago. Legends like the Four Horsemen are history you should know.

Ff

A field goal has been the difference in the final score of many Irish games. On the sideline, the placekicker must always be ready to enter the game and help the team. While the long snap from the center and the hold need to be accurate, the kicker must bear the pressure of performing successfully when the game is on the line and the chilly winds of South Bend are blowing.

F is for a Field Goal on a close game's final play.
The kicker gets three points for us and calmly saves the day.

G is for the Grotto, a place known
for peace and light.
For those who love Our Mother,
it's a blessed and holy site.

G g

The Notre Dame Grotto is perhaps the most visited and beloved place on campus. It is a one-seventh replica of the Grotto of Lourdes in France where Mary appeared to Saint Bernadette. Under the leadership of Reverend William Corby, C.S.C, the Grotto was completed in 1896. More than a century later, this quiet spot to light a candle and pray to the Blessed Mother still provides comfort and inspiration to students and visitors.

H h

H is for Hesburgh Library with the famous mural on its wall. When the Irish reach the end zone, arms are raised to make the call.

The Hesburgh Library, renamed in 1987 for Notre Dame President Emeritus Theodore Hesburgh, C.S.C., features Millard Sheets' *Word of Life* mural on the southern exterior wall. Towering over 134 feet high and 68 feet wide, Sheets' art depicts Jesus as teacher. The piece quickly became a favorite campus landmark, with fans dubbing the Christ with raised arms "Touchdown Jesus." Technically, the creation is neither mural nor mosaic, with 6,700 separate pieces of granite comprising this beautiful work of art.

I is for Inspiration drawn from a
teammate, family, or friend—
Especially for the great George Gipp,
a legend in South Bend.

I i

Many people have inspired Irish football players, but George Gipp is famous in Notre Dame lore. A complete player, Gipp led the team in rushing and passing in 1918, 1919, and 1920; kicked; and played flawless defense, never allowing a pass completion in his territory. Unfortunately, Gipp contracted strep throat and later pneumonia during his final season and died on December 14, 1920. Legend has it that while on his death bed, Gipp asked Rockne to remember him and sometime have the team "win just one for the Gipper." Rockne shared the conversation with his 1928 team during a halftime speech. The Irish responded by beating top-ranked Army 12-6. With the victory and a Hollywood retelling in the film *Knute Rockne All American*, the phrase "Win one for the Gipper" became a legendary part of Notre Dame football history.

J j

J is for the Jerseys, blue or white—or even green,

Which Dan Devine made famous with his winning "Green Machine."

Although the Irish primarily wear blue jerseys for home games and white for road games, many coaches, even Knute Rockne, have occasionally dressed the team in green. Dan Devine's surprise use of the color in 1977 helped to establish the current tradition of wearing green as a motivational tool. Basketball coach Digger Phelps urged Devine to consider using green jerseys when the football team faced heavily-favored USC. Devine agreed, letting only his captains know. The players hinted at the change during their pep rally speeches by referring to the team as the "Green Machine." After Notre Dame's 49-19 victory over the Trojans, the Irish wore green for the rest of the season and won the national championship. Today, the tradition of wearing green jerseys is often revived when Notre Dame is an underdog or the stakes of the game are especially high.

K is for the Kilts the Irish Guard wear on game day.
When the marching band takes the field, the Guard leads the way.

K k

The ten members of the Irish Guard, who have to be at least six foot two, wear a unique uniform that includes an Irish kilt in the Notre Dame plaid. Topped by tall bearskin hats, the Guard form an imposing presence when they lead the band across campus and onto the football field. Started in 1949, the Irish Guard originally played school songs on bagpipes, a practice that ended five years later. Today, both men and women who are tall enough can audition for a coveted spot in the Irish Guard during band camp week. If chosen, these students take their place at the head of the band.

L₁

Although the University officially adopted the nickname "The Fighting Irish" in 1927, the Leprechaun was not chosen as the school's mascot until 1965. Before then, a number of Irish terrier dogs had served in the role. Today, the Leprechaun is selected from the student body each year through a rigorous tryout process. Wearing a green suit and shaking a shillelagh, the Leprechaun leads the crowd in cheers at football games as well as other Notre Dame sporting events.

L is for the Leprechaun posed in his fighting stance.
When the Irish score, the fans will join him in a dance.

M is for the March through campus
the band will undertake
While thousands of Irish fans follow,
cheering in the wake.

Mm

The Fighting Irish Band's traditional march across campus is a memorable part of game day at Notre Dame. Over the years, the Band has met on the steps of Bond Hall or the Main Building, where they delight the gathering crowd with a mini-concert before "stepping off" for the game. From there, they lead scores of fans across campus to Notre Dame Stadium for pregame pageantry and the kickoff.

Nn

Being Number One is the goal of the Irish every year. In recent decades, an eight foot neon "1" sign adorns the top of Grace Hall when the Fighting Irish are the top-ranked team in the nation. This tradition started with a wooden version of the sign placed outside Moreau Seminary after the 1973 national championship. Notre Dame has finished with the top ranking and consensus national championship 11 times. The Irish ended up Number One in 1924, 1929, 1930, 1943, 1946, 1947, 1949, 1966, 1973, 1977, and 1988.

N is for being Number One, our team's yearly quest.
Eleven times the voters agreed the Irish were the best.

O is for the "1812 Overture" we'll hear.

Wave your arms with the students during this fourth-quarter cheer.

Oo

Just before the start of the fourth quarter, the Band of the Fighting Irish traditionally plays Pyotr Ilyich Tchaikovsky's "1812 Overture." Students and fans raise their arms and chop the air in unison. During Lou Holtz's tenure, students added a salute to their coach, forming an L with their thumb and index finger and chanting "Lou" on the downward stroke. The practice continues today with W's made to honor Coach Charlie Weis.

P p

In the midst of an exciting game, it is easy to forget that team members are young men who must balance the demands of rigorous classes with hours of practice, strength training, and film study. While the National Collegiate Athletic Association limits teams to 20 hours of player participation a week, the scholarship players, walk-ons, student managers, and student trainers who are a part of the program quickly find a lot of their day dedicated to football. State-of-the-art facilities like the Guglielmino Athletics Complex help make the busy lives of student-athletes easier; however, the players must still work diligently both on and off the field.

Practices should come to mind when we get to letter P,

For the Irish work hard all week long, not just the day we see.

Qq

Notre Dame has a history of outstanding quarterbacks. From Heisman Trophy winners Angelo Bertelli, Johnny Lujack, Paul Hornung, and John Huarte to NFL greats like Joe Theisman and Joe Montana, fans have witnessed talented generations of young men direct the Fighting Irish offense. Being the quarterback at Notre Dame comes with high expectations as fans are always looking for the next great Irish leader.

Q is for the Quarterbacks with strong arms and quick feet,
Leading the Irish with heart and skill, refusing to be beat.

R is for Knute Rockne, the winningest coach of all. With him, the Irish got their "fight" and started to pass the ball.

R r

Knute Rockne's contributions to Notre Dame and to college football cannot be overstated. As a football player, he was named a third-string end on Walter Camp's All-America team and served as a Notre Dame captain his senior year. Rockne also participated in track, drama, orchestra, and student publications—all while working as a janitor and chemistry research assistant to pay his tuition. A model student-athlete, Rockne graduated magna cum laude in 1914. As the head football coach from 1918 to 1930, Rockne compiled five undefeated seasons. His .881 winning percentage is still the highest in both the college and professional football ranks for coaches with 100 career victories. Rockne is also widely credited with creating lighter and more protective equipment and with implementing the forward pass as an equal component to the running game. His teams took on opponents across the country, earned respect with their dramatic victories, and gave the school a national fan base. The term "Fighting Irish" became a source of pride, and the school officially adopted it as the Notre Dame nickname during Rockne's tenure.

Rockne's accomplished life ended when he died in a plane crash on March 31, 1931 at the age of 43. The legacy he created is unparalleled in college football, and Knute Rockne remains one of Notre Dame's most revered and beloved men.

S is for the Students who stand and cheer the team along.
When the game is over, they sing our Blesse Mother's song.

The bond between the football players and their classmates is clearly visible on football Saturdays. Students remain standing for the entire game, and since the 1990s have embraced the tradition of wearing "The Shirt." Stretching from the 50-yard line to the end zone, the student sections provide an impressive vocal and visual support for the team. At the end of the game, players show their gratitude by raising their helmets to the student sections and joining their classmates for the playing of the "Notre Dame Victory March" and "Notre Dame, Our Mother," the University Alma Mater.

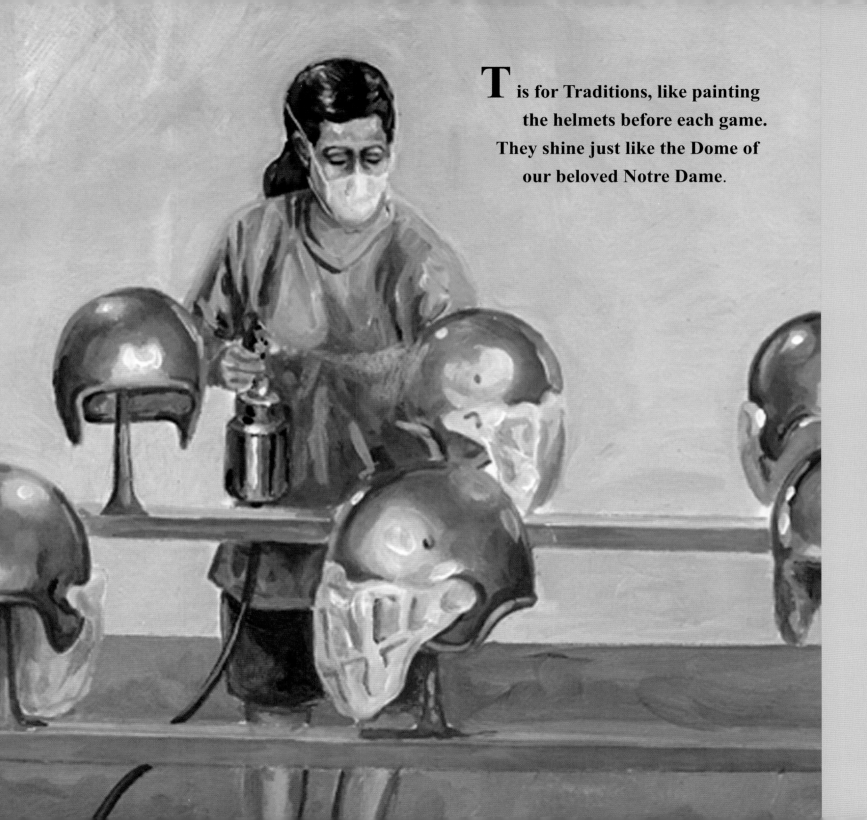

T is for Traditions, like painting
the helmets before each game.
They shine just like the Dome of
our beloved Notre Dame.

T t

The painting of the helmets is one of the most famous traditions surrounding Notre Dame football. Student managers repaint and buff the gold helmets every week, ensuring their special gleam on game day. The helmets' resemblance to the famous Golden Dome is no accident. Every few decades, the Dome is regilded, and the gold particles stripped off in the process are collected. The managers mix this gold dust with a paint gloss that becomes the final coat on the distinctive Notre Dame helmets.

U u

Many famous Notre Dame victories involved Irish teams that were seen as underdogs against undefeated opponents. Army, Georgia Tech, Oklahoma, Texas, USC, Miami, and Florida State all lost winning streaks of 16 games or more at the hands of the Irish. Sometimes, these unpredicted victories "wake up the echoes" and signal a return to prominence. Other times, they vault Notre Dame to a national championship. In every case, they reaffirm Notre Dame's stature as a formidable presence in college sports.

U is for being Underdogs. When the critics expect defeat,
The Irish stand tall and show the world they're still the team to beat.

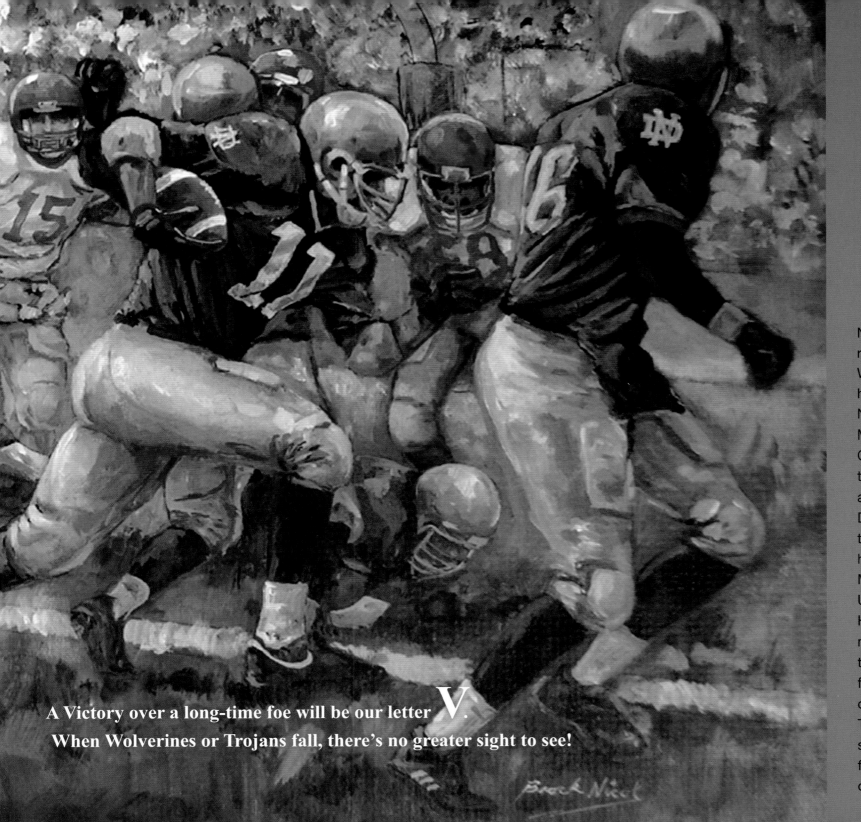

A Victory over a long-time foe will be our letter **V**.
When Wolverines or Trojans fall, there's no greater sight to see!

V v

Notre Dame has enjoyed spirited rivalries with many football teams. While the Fighting Irish share a history of memorable games with Navy, Army, Michigan State, and Miami, the victories against Southern California and Michigan are among the most celebrated triumphs of any season. Michigan and Notre Dame share the distinction of being the two winningest programs in the history of NCAA Division I football. Meanwhile, the match-up with USC, which has involved numerous Heisman Trophy winners and national title implications, remains the only true collegiate rivalry not fueled by geographical proximity or conference affiliation. With the Trojans and the Wolverines on the schedule for years to come, the Irish faithful can look forward to a future of classic gridiron battles.

W is for Walk-ons who rarely find glory or fame.
Their effort is for their teammates, their school,
and for the love of the game.

W
W

Each year, a group of dedicated young men earn spots on the Notre Dame football team as walk-ons. A few will be fortunate enough to earn scholarships, but the majority will devote enormous amounts of time and energy simply for the chance to play for the Fighting Irish. The 1993 film *Rudy* told the story of Daniel Reutigger, one such walk-on who found glory in a magical moment at Notre Dame Stadium. However, most walk-ons remain anonymous, working to make the team better without personal glory or significant playing time.

PLAY LIKE A CHAMPION TODAY

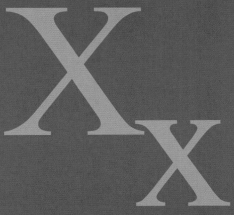

X is for the Exit players take before
  they play.
While going to the tunnel, they hit
  "Play Like a Champion Today."

The bright gold sign with the blue "Play Like a Champion Today" is now a deeply entrenched part of Notre Dame football. Coach Lou Holtz saw the phrase in Gerry Faust's office and envisioned using it as a motivational tool. Holtz had a sign bearing the phrase painted and hung at the exit from the football locker room to the stadium tunnel. Players quickly developed the practice of tapping the sign on their way to the field, a tradition that still exists today.

Y y

Many youngsters experience Notre Dame for the first time when they come to campus for a football game. Whether they attend the Blue-Gold game in the spring or are lucky enough to see a regular season contest, a first and lasting impression is often made. The shine of the Dome, the peace of the Grotto, the beauty of the campus, and the passion of the fans inspire youngsters to become lifelong fans, just like their parents.

Y is for the Youngsters here for their first game—like you—
And for your parents dreaming you'll be Domers one day, too.

Z z

Few teams in sports can claim a national following like Notre Dame enjoys. In every state and many countries around the world, scores of fans are gathered around radios, televisions, or internet broadcasts when the Irish take the field. With NBC televising home games since 1991, fans all over the country can share in the Notre Dame experience on a football Saturday.

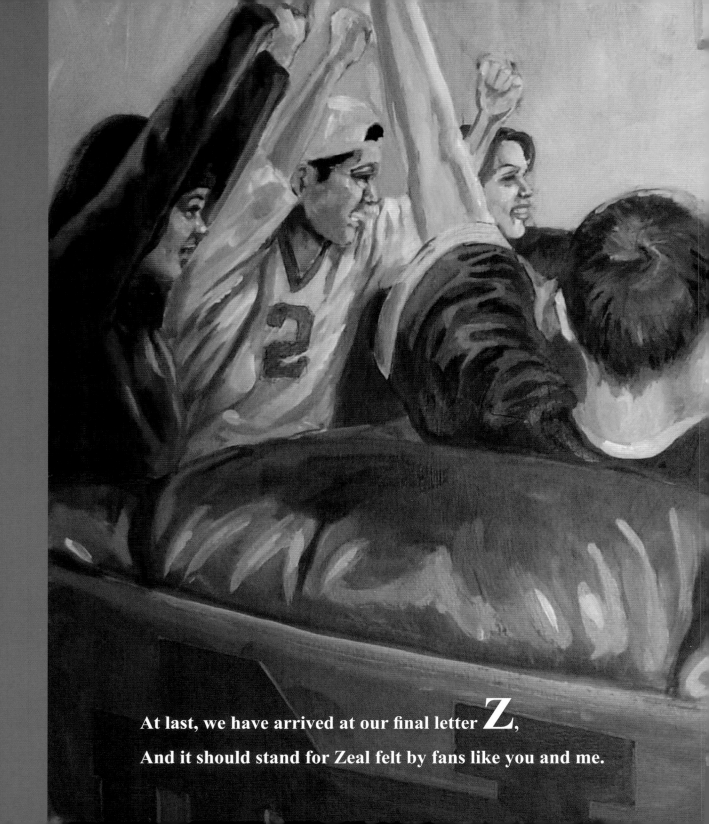

At last, we have arrived at our final letter Z,

And it should stand for Zeal felt by fans like you and me.

"Now I think we've done it," said my father with a grin,

"And I have talked enough, so let's go see the Irish win.

But someday when you're all grown up or when I'm far away,

I hope you will look back on this, our very special day.

Then go down to the Grotto, light a candle, say a prayer,

And go cheer on the Irish, knowing somehow I'll be there."